SO YOU THINK YOU KNOW... LIVERPOOL FC

James Redland

Copyright

'So you think you know…'

series of quiz books

2020

For Sue.

The biggest, littlest Liverpool fan I know.

Introduction

So you think you're a big Liverpool fan?

Well, now's your chance to prove it!

In this book you will find over 250 questions to tickle your brain cells. There are quotes, anagrams, song lyrics, pictures and trivia.

All of the questions have been thoroughly fact checked (on Google AND Wikipedia!) and are all correct as of January 2021.

If you are testing yourself then remember to cover the answers at the bottom of the page.

NO PEEKING!

Enjoy,

James

GENERAL KNOWLEDGE

Grab a pen and some paper, turn your brains to 'genius mode' and let's crack on…

QUIZ 1 – POT LUCK

1. In which year was Liverpool FC founded?

A. 1892   B. 1902   C. 1912

2. Who was the first manager of Liverpool FC?

3. How many fans watched the first game at Anfield in 1893?

A. 500   B. 5000   C. 15000

4. Which 2 colours made up Liverpool's kits for the first four years of their existence?

5. Who scored the first ever goal for LFC?

6. Which animal features on the club badge?

7. Fenway Sports, the current owners of LFC also own which other sports team?

8. Who is Liverpool's youngest goalscorer in a Premier League game?

9. What was the name of Liverpool's famous training ground until 2020?

10. Which nationality of player (after English) has most commonly represented LFC?

Answers: 1) 1892 2) John Mckenna 3) 5000 4) Blue and white 5) Malcolm McVean 6) The Liver bird 7) Boston Red Sox 8) Michael Owen 9) Melwood 10) Scotland

QUIZ 2 – TOP SCORERS

Can you name the top goal scorers from each of the last 20 seasons from just the player's first initial? Included is how many goals they scored in all competitions…

1) 19/20 – 23 goals – M_____

2) 18/19 – 27 goals – M_____

3) 17/18 – 44 goals – M_____

4) 16/17 – 14 goals – P_____

5) 15/16 – 13 goals – D_____

6) 14/15 – 13 goals – S_____

7) 13/14 – 31 goals – L_____

8) 12/13 – 30 goals – L_____

9) 11/12 – 17 goals – L_____

10) 10/11 – 15 goals – D_____

11) 09/10 – 22 goals – F_____

12) 08/09 – 24 goals – S_____

13) 07/08 – 33 goals – F_____

14) 06/07 – 18 goals – P_____

15) 05/06 – 23 goals – S_____

16) 04/05 – 13 goals – M_____

L_____

S_____

17. 03/04 – 19 goals – M_____

18. 02/03 – 28 goals – M_____

19. 01/02 – 29 goals – M_____

20. 00/01 – 24 goals – M_____

1) Mo Salah, 2) Mo Salah, 3) Mo Salah, 4) Phillipe Coutinho, 5) Daniel Sturridge 6) Steven Gerrard, 7) Luis Suarez 8) Luis Suarez 9) Luis Suarez, 10) Dirk Kuyt, 11) Fernando Torres, 12) Steven Gerrard, 13) Fernando Torres, 14) Peter Crouch, 15) Steven Gerrard, 16) Milan Baros, Luis Garcia and Steven Gerrard, 17) Michael Owen, 18) Michael Owen, 19) Michael Owen, 20) Michael Owen

QUIZ 3 – VIRGIL VAN DIJK

1. At which club did VVD start his senior career?
2. For how much did Liverpool sign him and from where?
3. How tall is he?
4. Which Scottish team did he play for between 2013 and 2015?
5. In which year did he make his full international debut?
   A. 2014   B. 2015   C. 2016
6. As of December 2020 how many goals has he scored for LFC?
   A. 5   B. 10   C. 20
7. Which striker said that he hated playing against VVD because he was 'too big, too strong, too quick and even smells good'?
8. His father is from the Netherlands but where is his mother from?
9. In October Van Dijk was injured when he collided with which player?
10. With who did Van Dijk score the most goals?
    A. Groningen   B. Celtic   C. Southampton

Answers: 1) Groningen 2) £75million from Southampton 3) 6foot 4 inches 4) Celtic 5) 2015 6) 10 goals 7) Troy Deeney 8) Suriname. 9) Jordan Pickford 10) Celtic

QUIZ 4 – ANAGRAMS

Can you work out who these players are from the past and the present? Included is the years they played for Liverpool.

1. Cavemans met man (90-99)
2. Rename cycle (67-81)
3. A mapped jerkin (91-02)
4. Snooty brander (17–present)
5. Manly job (84-96)
6. Coiled drunk (93-98)
7. Ammonia i knit mu (2020-present)
8. Hunger ort (58-69)
9. Advised jam (92-99)
10. Ash Ruin (80-86 and 88-96)

Answers: 1) Steve McManaman 2) Ray Clemence 3) Jamie Redknapp 4) Andy Robertson 5) Jan Molby 6) Neil Ruddock 7) Takumi Minamino 8) Roger Hunt 9) David James 10) Ian Rush

QUIZ 5 – RECORD BREAKERS

1. Who is Liverpool's leading goal scorer of all time?
2. Which midfielder scored Liverpool's fastest Premier League goal in 2019 when he netted in 15 seconds.
3. Liverpool's biggest Premier League win happened in December 2020. What was the score and who was it against?
4. What is the record attendance at Anfield?
   A. 55,985   B. 61,905   C. 70, 050
5. Roberto Firmino is the first Brazilian to score how many Premier League goals? (It's a round number).
6. As of December 2020 Liverpool have been undefeated for 64 league games at home. Who was the last team to beat Liverpool at Anfield in the Premier League?

7. Who has made the most appearances ever for LFC?
8. Which player had made the most European appearances having played in 150 games?
    A. Steven Gerrard.   B. Jamie Carragher
9. Which keeper has the most clean sheets ever for LFC?
10. In the title winning season of 19/20 what was the biggest points margin between first place Liverpool and second placed Man City?

Answers: 1) Ian Rush 2) Naby Keita 3) 7-0 vs Crystal Palace 4) 61,905 5) 50 6) Crystal Palace in April 2017 7) Ian Callaghan – 857 games 8) Jamie Carragher 9) Ray Clemence – 323. 10) 25

QUIZ 6 – STEVEN GERRARD

1. How many senior appearances did Steven Gerrard make for Liverpool?
   A. 550   B. 620   C. 709
2. What award did he win in 2006?
3. What shirt number is he most known for wearing?
4. In which Liverpool estate did he grow up?
5. Which MLS team to he go on to play for?
6. In the opening 18 games of the 20/21 Scottish Premiership how many games have Gerrard's Rangers team lost?
7. What is his middle name?
8. Who is he married to?
9. True or False – Gerrard made over 100 apearances for England
10. Name one of the four players that Gerrard stated were the best that he played with.

Answers: 1) 709. 2) MBE. 3) 8. 4) Huyton. 5) LA Galaxy 6) 0 7) George 8) Alex Curran 9) True 10) Xabi Alonso, Fernando Torres, Luis Suarez and Wayne Rooney

QUIZ 7 – GOALKEEPERS

1. Who was Liverpool's goalkeeper from 1981 to 1994?
2. Jerzy Dudek played for which national team?
3. Complete the name of the former keeper – Sander _____
4. True or False – Scott Carson only played 4 times for LFC.
5. Brad Friedel played for LFC across 4 years, name one of them.
6. Who played in goal for the 05/06 season?
7. Which country did Liverpool legend Bruce Grobbelaar represent?
8. Ned Doig is the oldest player to ever play for LFC. How old was he when he last played?
9. How many times did Ray Clemence play for LFC?
   A. 370   B. 420   C. 470
10. Which French keeper, signed from Leicester City made 2 appearances between 2000-2003?

Answers: 1) Bruce Grobbelaar. 2) Poland. 3) Westerveld. 4) True. 5) 97,98,99,2000. 6) Pepe Reina 7) Zimbabwe 8) 41 9) 470 10) Pegguy Arphexad

QUIZ 8 – ANFIELD

1. What are the names of the four stands that make up Anfield?
2. Which part of the stadium is named after Bill Shankly?
3. What is the name of the park that separates Anfield from Goodison Park?
4. What is the first part of the postcode for the stadium?
5. Which team played at the stadium between 1884 and 1891?
6. Who was responsible for installing the now famous 'This is Anfield' sign?
7. What is the capacity to the nearest thousand?
8. In what year was it converted to an all-seated stadium?
9. The Paisley Gateway includes the number of European trophies that the team won under Paisley. How many are there?
10.

Answers: 1) The Spion Kop, Anfield Road, Centenary and Sir Kenny Daglish. 2) The Shankly Gates 3) Stanley Park. 4) L4. 5) Everton. 6) Bill Shankly 7) 54,000 8) 1994 9) 3 10)

QUIZ 9 – PLAYER RATINGS

All of these questions are about the 20/21 team

Question 1 to 4 are according to FIFA 21 stats!

1. Who is the fastest player in the team with a Pace rating of 94?
   A. Mane   B. Virgil Van Dijk   C. Salah
2. Who has the best passing rating with 87?
   A. Robertson   B. Fabinho   C. Alexander-Arnold
3. Who has the lowest rating for shooting?
   A. Gomez   B. Robertson   C. Jones
4. 4 players have an overall rating of 90, how many can you name?
5. Who is the tallest player in the 20-21 team?
6. Who is the shortest?
7. Who is the oldest?
8. Who has the most international caps?
9. Who has the most international goals?
10. Who has the most Premier League appearances for Liverpool

Answers: 1) Sadio Mane 2) Alexander-Arnold 3) Gomez 4) Virgil Van Dijk, Mo Salah, Sadio Mane, Alisson 5) Virgil Van Dijk-6ft 3 6) Xherdan Shaqiri-5ft 5 7) James Milner-34 8) Xherdan Shaqiri-74 9) Mo Salah-29 10) Jordan Henderson-282

QUIZ 10 – ALL AROUND THE WORLD

LFC has fielded players from over 40 different countries. How many of these can you get?

1. Ronnie Rosenthal
2. Sami Hyypia
3. Daniel Agger
4. Patrick Berger
5. Martin Skrtel
6. Joel Matip
7. Naby Keita
8. Mohamed Sissoko
9. Sadio Mane
10. Alan Hansen

Answers: 1) Isreal 2) Finland 3) Denmark 4) Czech Republic 5) Slovakia 6) Cameroon 7) Guinea 8) Mali 9) Senegal 10) Scotland

QUIZ 11 – IAN RUSH

1. In which season did Ian Rush make his Liverpool debut?
2. In that season he made 9 appearances in all competitions. How many goals did he score?
   A. 0   B. 8   C. 13
3. For which national team did he play?
4. From which team did Liverpool sign him?
5. The fee paid was a record signing for a teenager, how much was paid for him?
   A. £100,000   B. £300,000   C. £500,000
6. Which Italian team bought Rush from Liverpool (before selling him back a season later)?
7. Which team did Rush manage in the 04/05 season?
8. How many goals did he score for Liverpool?
   A. 298   B. 346   C. 391
9. For how many seasons was Rush Liverpool's top scorer?
   A. 4   B. 8   C. 12
10. In a 2014 article Rush was credited with the 4th best what in football?

Answers: 1) 1980-1981. 2) 0. 3) Wales. 4) Chester City. 5) £300,000. 6) Juventus. 7) Chester City. 8) 346. 9) 8. 10) Moustache

QUIZ 12 – MO SALAH

1. Salah is known as the 'Egyptian' what?
2. Which premier league team did he play for between 2014–2016?
3. In his first season for Liverpool he played 52 games in all competitions, how many goals did he score?
A. 33   B. 37   C. 44
4. Salah played for 2 Italian teams, can you name them?
5. The fee paid for Salah was a club record. Whose record did it break?
6. True or False – Salah scored on his league debut
7. Which PFA award did he win in 2018?
8. True or False – he has scored more than 40 goals for Egypt
9. From which team did Chelsea sign Salah?
10. In which year was he born?

Answers: 1) King, 2) Chelsea, 3) 44, 4) Fiorentina and Roma, 5) Andy Carroll 6) True 7) PFA Player's Player of the Year 8) True 9) Basel 10) 1992

QUIZ 13 – MANAGERS

Can you name the last dozen managers from just the first initial? Each manager's win ratio is included. (Caretaker managers are not included, most recent first).

1. J_____ 61%
2. B_____ 50%
3. K_____ 47%
4. R_____ 42%
5. R_____ 55%
6. G_____ 52%
7. R_____ 52%
8. G_____ 42%
9. K_____ 60%
10. J_____ 54%
11. B_____ 58%
12. B_____ 52%

Answers: 1) Jurgen Klopp. 2) Brendan Rodgers. 3) Kenny Dagalish. 4) Roy Hodgson. 5) Rafael Benitez. 6) Gerard Houllier. 7) Roy Evans. 8) Graeme Souness. 9) Kenny Daglish. 10) Joe Fagan. 11) Bob Paisley. 12) Bill Shankly

QUIZ 14 – BILL SHANKLY

1. Which national team did Shankly represent as a player?
2. He only played for 2 club teams. 13 games for Carlisle United and 297 games for who?
3. For what reason was his career at Carlisle interrupted?
4. Which year did he become Liverpool manager?
   A. 1959   B. 1964   C. 1969
5. Who was Shankly's long time assistant at Liverpool?
6. Which division were Liverpool in when he took charge?
7. True or False – During Shankly's reign the club changed to an all red home strip and adopted You'll Never Walk Alone as the club anthem.
8. True or False – Shankly had 2 brothers who were all professional footballers.
9. How much was he paid per week during his playing days for Preston?
   A. £2   B. £5   C. £10
10. Can you name any of the teams he managed before Liverpool?

Answers: 1) Scotland 2) Preston North End 3) Service with the RAF during WW2 4) A 5) Bob Paisley 6) 2nd Division 7) True 8) False – he had 4, 9) £5 10) Carlisle United, Grimsby Town, Workington, Huddersfield Town

QUIZ 15 – BOB PAISLEY

1. True or False – Paisley spent his 35 years as part of Liverpool FC?
2. Who was Paisley's successor at Liverpool?
3. True or False – After leaving the post of Manager, Paisley took on the roles of reserve team coach and physiotherapist.
4. LFC won European Cups were won under his reign?
   A. 1   B. 3   C. 5
5. True or False – Paisley was said to have been reluctant to take on the role of Manager.
6. Who is the only manager who has won more honours per season?
   A. Alec Ferguson   B. Pep Guardiola   C. Jose Mourinho
7. Who was his first signing as Liverpool manager?
   A. Phil Neal   B. Peter McDonnell   C. Ray Kennedy
8. Liverpool set a club record when they beat Stromsgodset at Anfield in Paisley's 10th game in charge. What was the score?
   A. 11-0   B. 12-0   C. 18-0
9. Which defender, now a TV pundit, was Paisley's record signing costing £900,000 from Brighton and Hove Albion in 1981?
10. Who was the captain when Liverpool lifted their third League Cup under Bob Paisley in 1983?

Answers: 1) False, it was 44. 2) Joe Fagan 3) True 4) 3. 5) True 6) B 7) B 8) A 9) Mark Lawrenson 10) Graeme Souness

QUIZ 16 – MAGIC NUMBERS

Which squad number do the following players wear? (19/20 season)

1. Trent Alexander Arnold
2. Mo Salah
3. James Milner
4. Virgil Van Dijk
5. Sadio Mane
6. Naby Keita
7. Andy Robertson
8. Thiago Alcantara
9. Diogo Jota
10. Curtis Jones

Answers: 1) 66 2) 11 3) 7 4) 4 5) 10 6) 8 7) 26 8) 6 9) 20 10) 17

QUIZ 17 - BIGGEST TRANSFERS (IN)

Do you know who Liverpool's 25 most expensive signings are? Included is the transfer fee, the date of transfer and the club they were bought from.

1. 75 million – 2018 – Southampton
2. 56m – 2018 – Roma
3. 54m – 2018 – RB Leipzig
4. 41m – 2015 – Aston Villa
5. 40m – 2018 – AS Monaco
6. 37m – 2017 – Roma
7. 37m – 2016 – Southampton
8. 37m – 2015 – Hoffenheim
9. 37m – 2011 – Newcastle
10. 34m – 2007 – Athletico Madrid
11. 34m – 2017 – Arsenal
12. 28m – 2014 – Southampton

Answers: 1) Virgil Van Dijk 2) Alisson Becker 3) Naby Keita 4) Christian Benteke 5) Fabinho 6) Mo Salah 7) Sadio Mane 8) Bobby Firmino 9) Andy Carroll 10) Fernando Torres 11) Alex Oxlaide Chamberlain 12) Adam Lallana

13. 25m – 2016 – Newcastle

14. 24m – 2011 – Ajax

15. 23m – 2014 – Southampton

16. 23m – 2014 – Benfica

17. 22m – 2008 – Spurs

18. 20m – 2011 – Aston Villa

19. 20m – 2007 – West Ham United

20. 18m – 2009 – Portsmouth

21. 18m – 2014 – AC Milan

22. 18m – 2009 – Roma

23. 18m – 2004 – Auxerre

24. 17m – 2013 – PSG

25. 17m – 2012 - Swansea

Answers: 13) Gini Wijnaldum 14) Luis Suarez 15) Dejan Lovren 16) Lazar Markovic 17) Robbie Keane 18) Stewart Downing 19) Javier Mascherano 20) Glen Johnson 21) Mario Balotelli 22) Alberto Aquilani 23) Djibril Cisse 24) Mamadou Sakho 25) Joe Allen

QUIZ 18 - TRENT AND ROBBO

1. What year were both players born? (not the same year).
2. In which city was Andy Robertson born?
3. And with which team did he start his career?
4. What is Trent Alexander Arnold's middle name?
   A. John   B. Kevin   C. Dave
5. True or False – TAA could've qualified to play for the USA through his grandma.
6. Who has more Premier League assists in total?
7. And who is taller?
8. Who was Liverpool's predominant right back before Trent's emergence?
9. How much did Liverpool pay for Andy Robertson?
10. From which team was he bought?

Answers: 1) Robbo – 1994, TAA - 1998 2) Glasgow 3) Queen's Park 4) John 5) True 6) Andy Robertson – 37 vs TAA - 28 7) Andy Robertson 5ft 10, TAA – 5ft 9. 8) Nathaniel Clyne 9) 8m 10) Hull City

QUIZ 19 - JOHN BARNES

1. In which year did Barnes make his debut for Liverpool?
2. In which country was he raised until the age of 12?
3. From which team was he signed?
4. Name the song that Barnes performed a 'rap' on?
5. Which manager signed Barnes for Liverpool?
6. True or False – the fee paid exceeded £1 million.
7. Barnes finished as the clubs second highest goalscorer in his first season. Who did he finish second to?
    A. Peter Beardsley   B. Kenny Daglish
    C. John Aldridge
8. In his entire Liverpool career do you think he scored more or fewer goals than he assisted?
9. How many international caps did he win?
    A. 39   B. 59   C. 79
10. Barnes went on to manage 3 teams for brief spells. Can you name one of them?

Answers: 1) 1987 2) Jamaica 3) Watford 4) World in Motion 5) Kenny Daglish 6) False – it was £900,000 7) John Aldridge 8) More – 108 goals vs 101 assists 9) 79 10) Celtic, Jamaica and Tranmere Rovers

QUIZ 20 - BIGGEST TRANSFERS (OUT)

Can you name the biggest transfers to leave LFC?

1. 142 million – 2018 - Barcelona

2. 75m – 2014 – Barcelona

3. 50m – 2011 – Chelsea

4. 49m – 2015 – Man City

5. 32m – 2016 – Crystal Palace

6. 30m – 2009 – Real Madrid

7. 26m – 2017 – Crystal Palace

8. 23.5m – 2020 – Sheffield United

9. 20m – 2019 – Southampton

10. 19m – 2019 - Bournemouth

Answers: 1) Philippe Coutinho 2) Luis Suarez 3) Fernando Torres 4) Raheem Sterling 5) Christian Benteke 6) Xabi Alonso 7) Mamadou Sakho 8) Rhian Brewster 9) Danny Ings 10) Dominic Solanke

WHO SAID IT?

There have been many profound things said about Liverpool over the years, and some less so.

Can you name who said the following…

Who said –

THE BEST FOOTBALL IS ABOUT EXPRESSION OF EMOTION. ALWAYS.

Jurgen Klopp

Who said –

THIS CITY HAS TWO GREAT TEAMS – LIVERPOOL AND LIVERPOOL RESERVES.

Bill Shankly

Who said :-

THIS CLUB HAS BEEN MY LIFE. I'D GO OUT AND SWEEP THE STREET AND BE PROUD TO DO IT FOR LIVERPOOL FC IF THEY ASKED ME TO.

Bob Paisley

Who said –

WHEN I DIE, DON'T BRING ME TO HOSPITAL. BRING ME TO ANFIELD. I WAS BORN THERE AND WILL DIE THERE.

Steven Gerrard

Who said –

LIVERPOOL FC IS NOT JUST A FOOTBALL CLUB, IT'S A WAY OF LIFE.

Kenny Dalglish

Who said –

THERE ARE THOSE WHO SAY MAYBE I SHOULD FORGET ABOUT FOOTBALL. MAYBE I SHOULD FORGET ABOUT BREATHING.

Gerard Houllier

Who said –

I JUST COULDN'T SETTLE IN ITALY. IT WAS LIKE LIVING IN A FOREIGN COUNTRY.

Ian Rush

Who said –

IF EVERTON WERE PLAYING AT THE BOTTOM OF THE GARDEN, I'D PULL THE CURTAINS.

Bill Shankly

Who said –

THEY COMPARE STEVE MCMANAMAN TO STEVE HEIGHWAY AND HE'S NOTHING LIKE HIM, BUT I CAN SEE WHY – IT'S BECAUSE HE'S A BIT DIFFERENT.

Kevin Keegan

Who said –

IF LIVERPOOL FC PLAYED A CUP FINAL ON THE MOON OUR FANS WOULD FIND A WAY OF GETTING THERE.

Steven Gerrard

WHO AM I?

Can you help me out please? I have COMPLETELY forgotten who I am. I can, however, remember every team I played for (which is convenient). There are some pictures in here too.

Who am I?

I was born in 1975 and played for: Liverpool, Leeds, Man City and Perth Glory, amongst others.

Robbie Fowler

Who am I?

I was born in 1981 and played for: Real Sociedad, Liverpool, Real Madrid and Bayern Munich.

Xabi Alonso

Who am I?

I was born in 1968. I played left back for: West Bromwich Albion, Liverpool, West Ham, Everton, Coventry, Birmingham City and Sheffield Wednesday.

David Burrows

Who am I?

Steven Gerrard

Who am I?

Mo Salah

Who am I?

John Barnes

Who am I?

Joe Gomez

Who am I?

"I was born in 1947. I played for Blackpool, Liverpool, Wolves, Rotherham, Hull and Swansea. I racked up 665 games for LFC and also played for England."

Emlyn Hughes

Who am I?

"I was born in 1963. I played for: Kolding, Ajax, Liverpool, Barnsley, Norwich and Swansea City."

Jan Molby

Who am I?

Pepe Reina

Who am I?

Ian Rush

Who am I?

"I was born in 1968 in London. I spent most of my career playing for various London teams but I played 115 games in defence for LFC. I have a sharp sounding nickname."

Neil 'Razor' Ruddock

Who are we?

Answers: from left to right – Trent Alexander Arnold, Jordan Henderson, Andy Robertson

MISSING MEN

Can you work out who's missing from the following team sheets…

MISSING MEN - 2005 vs AC Milan

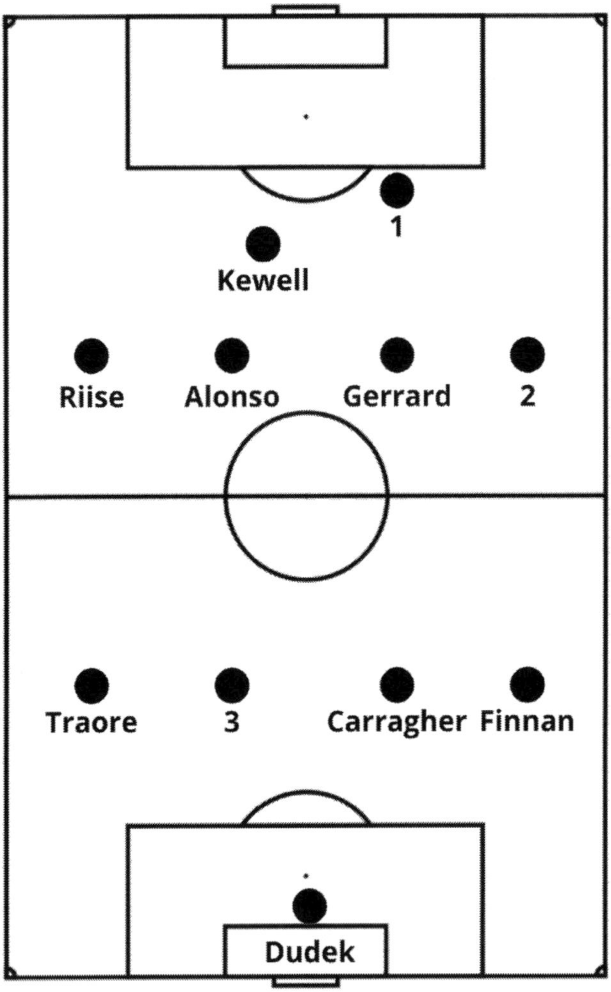
1
Kewell
Riise
Alonso
Gerrard
2
Traore
3
Carragher
Finnan
Dudek

Answers: 1) Baros 2) Garcia 3) Hyypia

MISSING MEN - 2009 vs Burnley

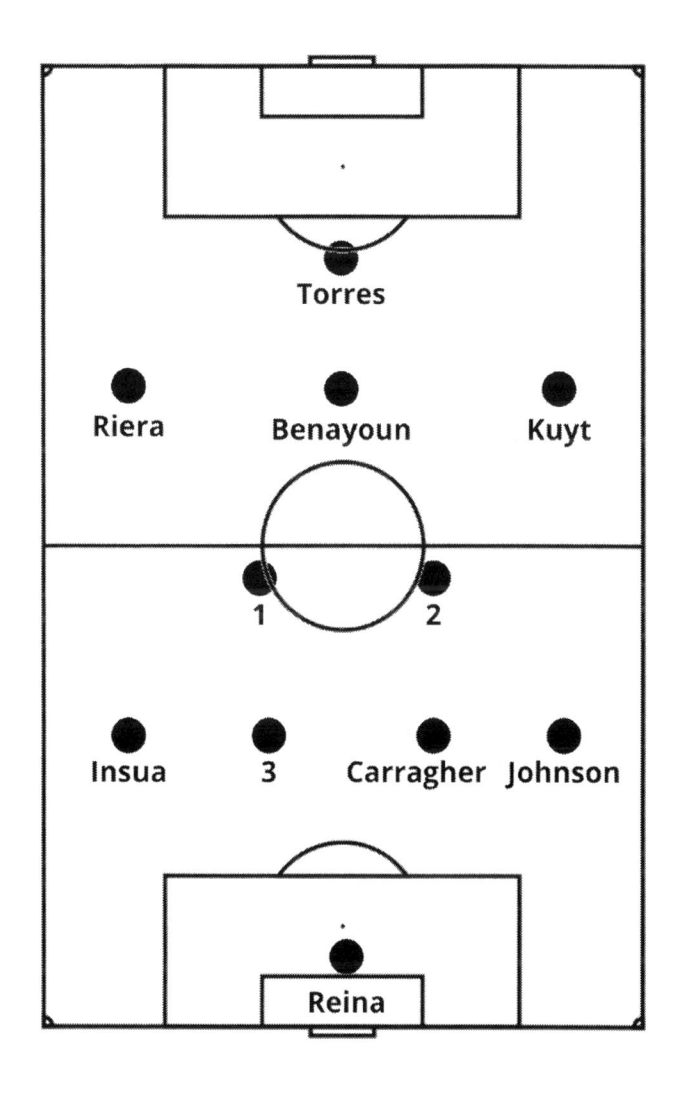

Torres

Riera   Benayoun   Kuyt

1   2

Insua   3   Carragher   Johnson

Reina

Answers: 1) Gerrard 2) Lucas 3) Skrtel

MISSING MEN - 1989 vs Everton

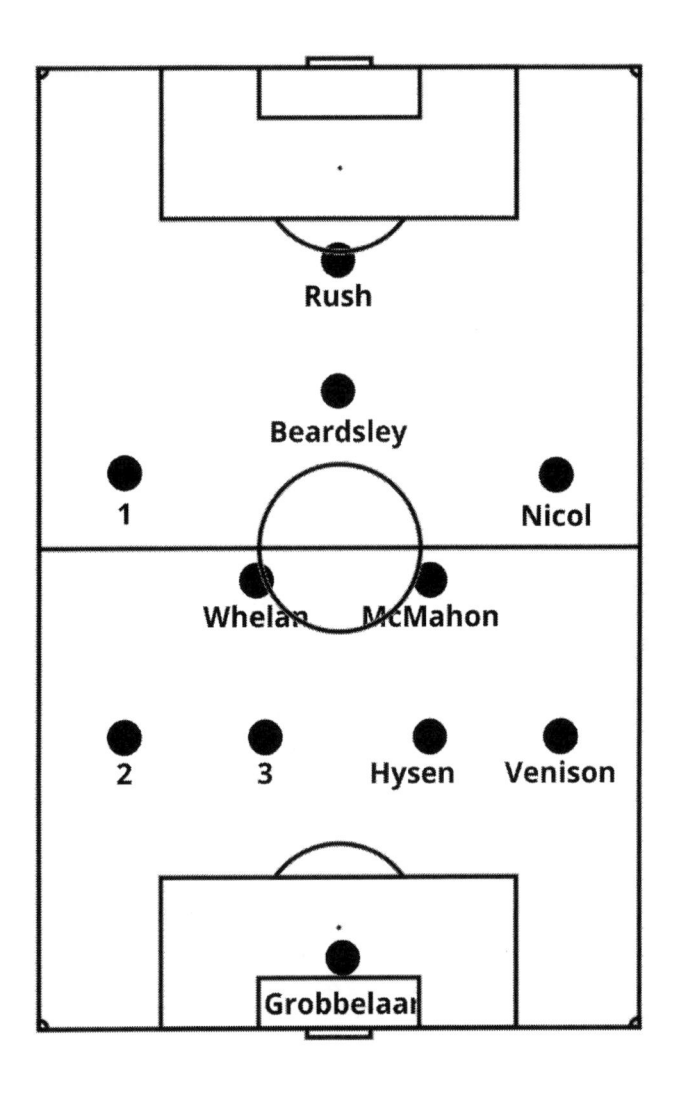

Rush

Beardsley

1 Nicol

Whelan McMahon

2 3 Hysen Venison

Grobbelaar

Answers: 1) Barnes 2) Burrows 3) Hansen

MISSING MEN - 1998 vs Newcastle

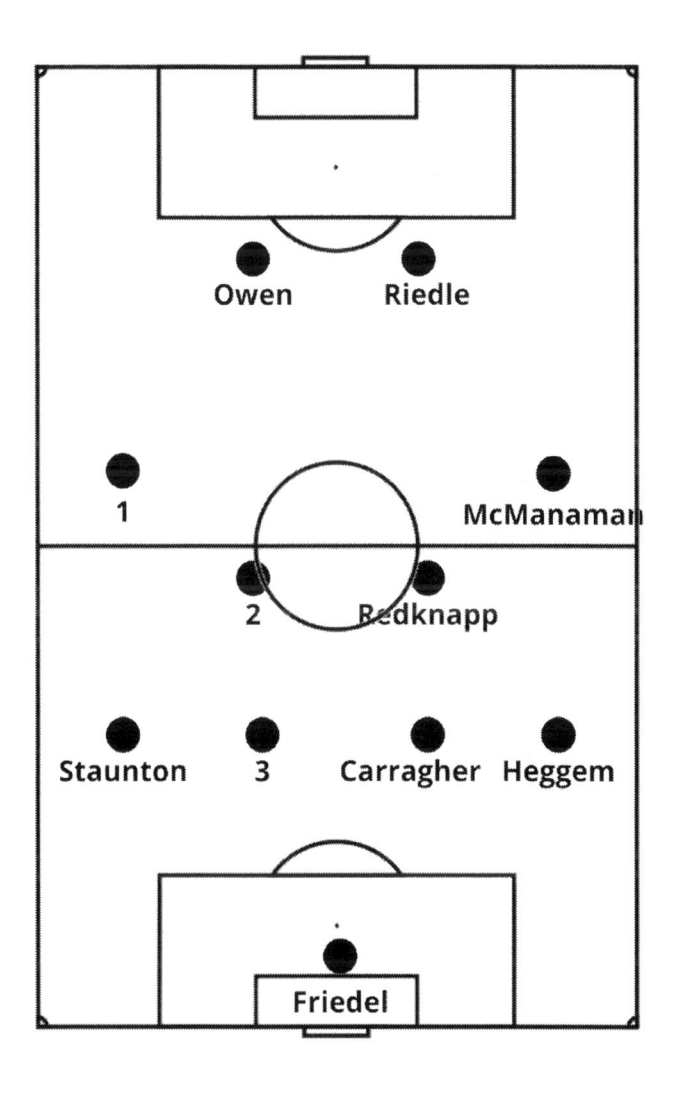

Owen Riedle

1 McManaman

2 Redknapp

Staunton 3 Carragher Heggem

Friedel

Answers: 1) Berger 2) Ince 3) Babb

MISSING MEN - 2003 vs Spartak

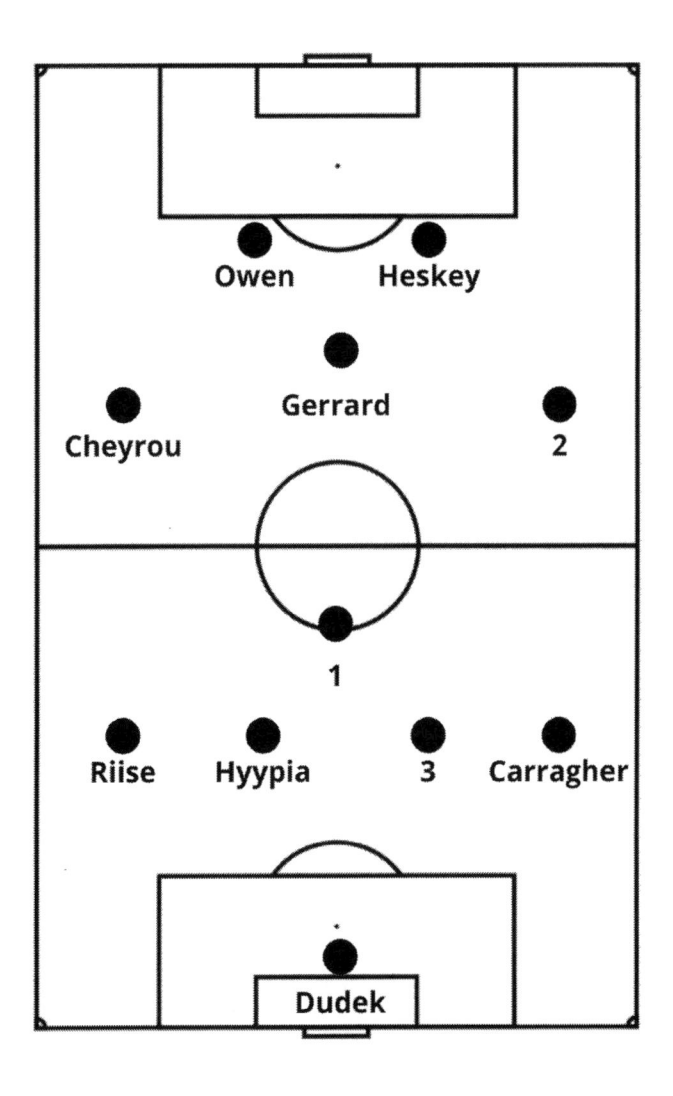

Owen   Heskey

Gerrard

Cheyrou   2

1

Riise   Hyypia   3   Carragher

Dudek

Answers: 1) Hamann 2) Murphy 3) Henchoz

THE FA CUP

Liverpool have won the FA Cup 7 times. Can you work out the scorers from each Cup Final?

I've include the first initial of the players surname, because I'm nice like that.

And also the minute that they scored in (like that will help).

1965 FA CUP FINAL

Liverpool 2
Leeds United 1

LFC scorers:
H_ _ _ (93)
S_ _ _ _ _ (117)

Leeds Utd scorer:
B_ _ _ _ _ _ (100)

Answers: Hunt, St John, Bremner

1974 FA CUP FINAL

Liverpool 3
Newcastle United 0

LFC scorers:

K _ _ _ _ _ (57, 88)

H _ _ _ _ _ _ _ (74)

Answers: Keegan, Heighway

1974 FA CUP FINAL

Liverpool 3
Newcastle United 0

LFC scorers:
K _ _ _ _ _ (57, 88)
H _ _ _ _ _ _ _ (74)

Answers: Keegan, Heighway

1986 FA CUP FINAL

Liverpool 3
Everton 1

LFC scorers:

R _ _ _ (56, 83)

J _ _ _ _ _ _ _ (62)

Everton Scorer:

L _ _ _ _ _ (27)

Answers: Rush, Johnston, Lineker

1989 FA CUP FINAL

Liverpool 3
Everton 2

LFC scorers:

A _ _ _ _ _ _ _ (4)

R _ _ _ (68, 104)

Everton Scorers:

M _ _ _ _ (90, 102)

Answers: Aldridge, Rush, McCall

1992 FA CUP FINAL

Liverpool 2
Sunderland 0

LFC scorers:
T_ _ _ _ _ (47)
R_ _ _ (68)

Answers: Thomas, Rush

2001 FA CUP FINAL

Liverpool 2
Arsenal 1

LFC scorers:
O_ _ _ (83, 88)

Arsenal scorer:
L_ _ _ _ _ _ _ _ (72)

Answers: Owen, Ljungberg

2006 FA CUP FINAL

Liverpool 3
West Ham United 3

(Liverpool win 3-1 on penalties)

LFC scorers:

C_ _ _ _ (32)

G_ _ _ _ _ _ (54, 90)

West Ham scorers:

C_ _ _ _ _ _ _ _ _ (21 og)

A_ _ _ _ _ (28)

K_ _ _ _ _ _ _ _ (64)

Answers: Cisse, Gerrard, Carragher, Ashton, Konchesky

THE EUROPEAN CUP/ UEFA CHAMPIONS LEAGUE

Just the six times for this one…

1977 EUROPEAN CUP FINAL
Stadio Olimpico, Rome

Liverpool 3
Borussia Monchengladbach 1

LFC scorers:

MC _ _ _ _ _ _ _ (28)

S _ _ _ _ (64)

N _ _ _ (82, pen)

Borussia Monchengladbach scorers:

Simonsen (52)

Answers: McDermott, Smith, Neal

1978 EUROPEAN CUP FINAL
Wembley Stadium, London

Liverpool 1
Club Brugge 0

LFC scorer:
D _ _ _ _ _ (64)

Answers: Dalglish

1981 EUROPEAN CUP FINAL
Parc des Princes, Paris

Liverpool 1
Real Madrid 0

LFC scorer:
K _ _ _ _ _ (82)

Answers: Kennedy

1984 EUROPEAN CUP FINAL
Stadio Olimpico, Rome

Liverpool 1
Roma 1
Liverpool won 4-2 on penalties

LFC scorer:

N _ _ _ (13)

Roma scorer

Pruzzo (42)

Answers: Neal

2005 CHAMPIONS LEAGUE FINAL
Ataturk Olympic Stadium, Istanbul

Liverpool 3
Milan 3
Liverpool won 3-2 on penalties

LFC scorers:

G _ _ _ _ _ _ (54)

S _ _ _ _ _ (56)

A _ _ _ _ _ (60)

Milan scorers:

M _ _ _ _ _ _ (1)

C _ _ _ _ _ (39, 44)

Answers: Gerrard, Smicer, Alonso, Maldini, Crespo

2019 CHAMPIONS LEAGUE FINAL
Metropolitano Stadium, Madrid

Liverpool 2
Tottenham Hotspur 0

LFC scorers:

S _ _ _ _ (2)

O_ _ _ _ (87)

Answers: Salah, Origi

SONG LYRICS

The Kop is known the world over for its songs but how well do you know the lyrics?

Complete the lyrics –

There's something that the _____ want you to know,

The best in the world is _____ _____

Our number nine,

Give him the ball and he will score every time.

_____

Give the ball to _____ and he will score.

Answers: Kop, Bobby Firmino, Si Senor, Bobby

Who is the subject of this song?

He's big, he's red, his feet stick out the bed.

Peter Crouch

Complete the lyrics –

He's our centre-half
He's number four
Watch him _____
And watch him _____
He'll pass the ball
Calm as you like
He's _____ ___ ___
He's _____ ___ ___

Answers: defend, score, Virgil Van Dijk, Virgil Van Dijk

Complete the lyrics –

We've conquered all of _____,
We're never gonna stop,
From _____ on to _____,
We've won the flipping lot!

____ _____ and ____ _____,
The fields of Anfield Road,
We are loyal supporters,
We come from Liverpool!

Allez, allez, allez!
Allez, allez, allez!
Allez, allez, allez!
Allez, allez, allez!

Answers: Europe, Paris, Turkey, Bob Paisley, Bill Shankly

Complete the lyrics -

When you walk through a _____,
Hold your head up high
And don't be afraid of the dark
At the end of the storm,
there's a _____ sky
And the sweet, silver song of a _____

Walk on through the wind
Walk on through the rain
Though your _____ be tossed
and blown

Walk on, walk on
With hope in your _____
And you'll never walk alone
You'll never walk alone

Answers: storm, golden, lark, dreams, heart

Complete the lyrics -

His armband proved his was a red.

_____, _____

You'll never walk alone _____

_____

_____, _____

We bought the lad from sunny

_____

He gets the ball and scores again.

Fernando Torres!

Liverpool's number _____!

Answers: Torres, Torres, it, said, Torres, Torres, Spain, nine

Complete the lyrics -

Saturday night, and I like the way you move,

_____

_____

Answers: Dinock Origi

IN WHICH SEASON DID THESE THINGS HAPPEN?

Which season is this?

- Liverpool finished as champions and won the FA Cup
- Ian Rush scored 31 goals
- Kenny Daglish took charge as manager

1985/86

Which season is this?

- Liverpool finished third in the league
- They won the FA Cup and the UEFA Super Cup
- Steven Gerrard finished as top scorer

2005/06

Which season is this?

- Bill Shankly led Liverpool to fifth place in the league
- Roger Hunt finished as top scorer with 19 goals
- England did quite well in the World Cup! (Of which Hunt, Ian Callaghan and Gerry Byrne were members of the squad.)

1966/67

Which season is this?

- Jurgen Klopp became manager
- Liverpool finished 8th in the league
- Daniel Sturridge finished as top goal scorer in all competitions with 13 goals.

Which season is this?

- Bob Paisley took charge
- Steve Heighway finished as top scorer in all competitions with 13 goals
- Liverpool finished 2nd in the league

1974/75

DID YOU KNOW?

Amaze your friends with your knowledge!

Did you know?

Sadio Mane holds the record for the fastest Premier League hat-trick. The previous record was held by Robbie Fowler.

Did you know?

The Kop is named after a hill in South Africa where the Boer War took place.

Did you know?

Kenny Daglish was the first ever player-manager in English football

Did you know?

In the 2001-2002 season defender Abel Xavier played one Merseyside derby game for Liverpool and one for Everton.

Did you know?

The Kop has a capacity of 12,500 but when spectators were standing it held 30,000

Did you know?

Ian Callaghan holds the record for most appearances and was only booked ONCE in 857 games for the club!

Did you know?

Melwood was named after two priests, Father Melling and Father Woodlock.

Did you know?

Liverpool's honours list is:

19 times League Title winners

6 times European Cup winners

3 times UEFA Cup winners

4 times European Super Cup winners

1 time Club World Cup winners

7 times FA Cup winners

8 times Football League Cup winners

15 times Charity/Community shield winners

And finally...

Liverpool are one of 5 English teams to begin and end with the same letter. Can you name the other 4?

Answers: Aston Villa, Charlton Athletic, Northampton Town, York City

So, how did you get on?

Are you as big a fan as you thought?

If you have enjoyed this book then please leave a review on Amazon and check out the others in the series!

Thanks,

James